Ulysses S. Grant

Ulysses S.
GRANT

Bill Bentley

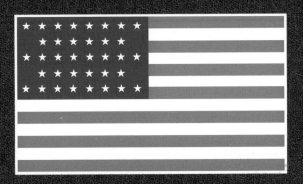

Franklin Watts
New York / Chicago / London / Sydney
A First Book

Map by Donald Charles
Photographs copyright ©: cover, 20, 33: Library of Congress; 2, 12, 22 (top), 27, 28, 34, 38, 40, 41, 46, 47, 48, 52, 53, 55: The Bettmann Archive; 3, 8: © Whitney Smith, Flag Research Center; 9: Steve Solum/Third Coast Stock Sources; 11, 21: Historical Pictures/Stock Montage; 15, 16: West Point Museum, U.S. Military Academy, New Point, NY; 19, 49, 57: North Wind Picture Archives; 22 (bottom), 25, 30, 36, 56: Chicago Historical Society; 31, 39, 42, 43, 50: Culver Pictures; 37 (top): Peter Pearson/Tony Stone Images; 37 (bottom): Galena State Historic Sites, Illinois Historic Preservation Agency; 44: National Portrait Gallery, Washington, DC/Art Resource, NY; 58: Andy Levin/Photo Researchers

Library of Congress Cataloging-in-Publication Data
Bentley, Bill.
Ulysses S. Grant / by Bill Bentley.
p. cm. — (A First book)
Includes bibliographical references (p.) and index.
Summary: A biography of the commander of the Union forces in the Civil War who became the eighteenth president of the United States.
ISBN 0-531-20162-7 (lib. bdg.)
1. Grant, Ulysses S. (Ulysses Simpson), 1822-1885—Juvenile literature. 2. Presidents—United States—Biography—Juvenile literature. 3. Generals—United States—Biography—Juvenile literature. 4. United States. Army—Biography—Juvenile literature. [1. Grant, Ulysses S. (Ulysses Simpson), 1822-1885. 2. Presidents.] I. Title. II. Series.
E672.B44 1993 973.8'2'092—dc20
[B] 93-416 CIP AC

Contents

To my daughters, Linda and Libby.

Chapter One

BOYHOOD
AND
GROWING UP

TWO THINGS HAPPENED on April 27, 1822, in Point Pleasant, Ohio. Jesse and Hannah Grant had a new son, and the United States had a future great general and president of the United States.

The Grants, like most people in this quiet pioneer settlement, were from families that had emigrated from Pennsylvania. Jesse and Hannah had met in Point Pleasant and were married after an extended courtship. A year later their first child was born, and after much discussion among relatives the boy was baptized Hiram Ulysses Grant.

Ulysses was a combination of his parents' traits. Jesse, talkative and inclined to brag, was a good businessman with

Grant's birthplace,
Pleasant Point, Ohio

a reputation for being honest in all of his transactions. Ulysses also inherited his father's confidence and determination, and an intense desire to finish something once it was started. This quality of not turning back was destined to play an important part in Ulysses' later life and would help him over many rough spots in his military career.

Ulysses' mother, Hannah, was the opposite of Jesse. Quiet and reserved, she was not one to display her emotions. Both she and Jesse set fine examples for their six children, and while not highly educated themselves, they both realized the value of an education and trained their children accordingly.

Ulysses was born in a time when opportunities were few and money was scarce. In those days, a child carried much responsibility. At the age of seven, instead of playing games with his friends, Ulysses would be hauling wagon loads of wood, plowing the fields, and performing other tasks generally done by men.

Ulysses' education, like most of the other children who attended frontier settlement schools, was limited to the most basic subjects. While the early settlers who came to the Ohio region no doubt would have liked better schools, they had to be content with the quality of schools and teachers they were able to secure. The majority of the schools in those days were called log schools and were often built in one day, from top to bottom.

Grant's parents, Jesse R. Grant and
Hannah Grant

The schoolhouse in Georgetown, Ohio,
where Grant was educated as a child

When he was ten, Ulysses already had a reputation for handling horses well. When people came to the Grants' livery stable to hire transportation to other cities, Ulysses often drove the horses from their home in Georgetown, Ohio, to Cincinnati or Louisville. The passengers were sometimes hesitant about hiring a little boy to drive them more than 40 miles (64 km), but there would always be plenty of people around to say that Ulysses was capable of handling the situation.

By the time Ulysses had reached the age of twelve he had become an excellent horseman. Even horse-traders who wanted to show a horse's speed sought his services as a rider. Colts who had never felt a saddle were handed over to Ulysses for "breakin' in."

Ulysses also worked with his father in the Grants' tannery (a place where animal hides were turned into leather). One of his main tasks was in the "bark mill," where bark was ground and used in the tanning process. Ulysses drove a horse hitched to a pole that was connected to a wide sweep. The horse would walk in a circle pushing the pole, thus supplying force to grind the bark. Ulysses' job was to keep the horse moving while another boy broke strips of bark with a hammer and fed the bark into the millhopper. Ulysses thought he had the better job of the two because he was able to ride a horse!

Ulysses tried his hand at other jobs in the tannery but realized that he did not want to make this his life's work. He really wanted a good education, and he thought he would become a farmer or river trader.

Being an obedient and hard working son, Ulysses was seldom scolded by his parents, and they permitted him a great deal of freedom to do what he wished in the little free time he could manage. He liked to ride, fish, or swim in the summer and ice skate in the winter. As the oldest child in the family, he possessed a great deal of confidence in his ability to take care of himself.

As a young man starting to think about a career, Ulysses realized the benefits of a college education. His father suggested various occupations, but nothing appealed to Ulysses except an education at West Point, the United States Military Academy. Ulysses was not so interested in the military, but an education there could open up opportunities for him in engineering or business. Luckily for Ulysses, a West Point vacancy did occur and through the efforts of his father, who kept pushing Congressman Hamer of Ohio, Ulysses' name was submitted as a candidate, and he was readily accepted.

Chapter Two

WEST POINT

FIFTEEN DAYS AFTER leaving Ohio, Ulysses arrived at West Point, having stopped along the way in Pittsburgh, Harrisburg, Philadelphia, and New York City. The steamboat that carried him the final 40 miles (64 km) up the Hudson River came to a stop at the river's edge, and Ulysses certainly must have gazed with wonder at the scenic heights of Storm King Mountain that formed a background for the United States Military Academy.

This was a big moment in his life—he had finally arrived at West Point. But he was faced with an immediate challenge. Before being officially admitted to West Point, all cadets had to pass rigorous entrance examinations.

West Point, the United States Military
Academy. Grant graduated from West Point in
1843 as a second lieutenant.

Ulysses was seventeen when he entered West Point and had not had the intensive early study that most of the other cadets had received. The tests did cover material he had studied in the common schools back in Ohio, and although it was an arduous test, Ulysses passed.

Ulysses' appointment papers caused his military career to begin in a confusion of names. Congressman Hamer had made a mistake in filling out Ulysses' papers and listed the boy's name as Ulysses Simpson Grant, not Hiram Ulysses. The congressman had known the Grants' son back in Georgetown as Ulysses and had supposed that his middle name was Simpson, Mrs. Grant's maiden name. To avoid complications, Ulysses just signed the official records, U.S. Grant, the name he would be known by throughout his life.

As America's needs for canals, roads, railroads, and the development of waterways increased, so did the demands for West Point graduates. They were eagerly sought after in civil life to take the lead in railway engineering and industrial pursuits. While much emphasis was put upon civil engineering, the fact was never forgotten that the academy's main purpose was to train its graduates in the art and science of war.

Selecting what subjects to take at West Point did not present a problem for Cadet Grant, because, like other cadets, his course work was mapped out for him. The subjects included Infantry Drill, Construction of Field Works, and Fortifications.

As a scholar, Ulysses was not particularly outstanding, but he plodded along slowly in his studies and proved himself a good thinker who would stay with a problem until it was finished. Mathematics was his favorite subject.

From the time he entered the academy until the day he graduated, cadet life was one continuous timetable for Ulysses. Cadets were awakened at five o'clock each morning by the roll of drums, then a brisk march to the mess hall for breakfast. After this they attended classes for five hours before returning to the dining room for lunch. The afternoons and early evenings were occupied by drill and recreation, followed by the evening meal and then "lights out" at 10:00 P.M.

Inspections for the cadets were extremely strict. Barracks rooms, with their simple tables and chairs, had to be spotless. Uniforms, shoes, insignias had to be perfect, as even the smallest mistake would earn a demerit that had to be worked off by marching with a rifle and pack for a required amount of time.

In his early years as a cadet, Ulysses did not carry the appearance of a military man. The hard work he did as a boy had given him a stooped look, and his West Point training eventually helped him overcome this. In fact, when he went home for his only visit in his four years at West Point, the first thing that caught his mother's eye was his more rugged look and gentlemanly appearance.

West Point cadets performing
exercises on horseback

Ulysses was popular with the other cadets because of his honesty, fair dealings, and respect for the rights of others. They gave him the nickname of "Sam Grant" in reference to the U.S. (Uncle Sam) part of his name. The cadet corps also recognized his ability as a bold and fearless rider, one of the best to ever attend West Point.

Chapter Three

WAR DRUMS

ULYSSES GRANT GRADUATED from West Point in 1843 as a second lieutenant. He ranked twenty-first in a class of thirty-nine. Because of his experience with horses he had hoped for an assignment with the cavalry. Instead, Grant was ordered to report to the 4th Infantry based at Jefferson Barracks, a well-known military post near St. Louis, Missouri. Although he was not happy with the assignment, he put his disappointment aside and began serving with his new outfit. There was something that he could not know when he arrived at Jefferson Barracks in 1843—it was there that he would meet his future bride,

Julia Dent, whose brother, Fredrick, had been one of Ulysses' closest friends at West Point.

Lieutenant Grant would not have to wait long before seeing action and battle experience. A dispute over the Texas–Mexico border turned violent with the arrival of the U.S. Army, and the Mexican War had begun. Grant went to war with the 4th Infantry and distinguished himself through several acts of bravery. The war eventually ended on September 14, 1847, when the United States captured

Ulysses S. Grant as a lieutenant in the Mexican War, 1846

Above, Julia Dent Grant,
Grant's wife.
Right, The Grant &
Perkins leather store,
where Grant worked after
leaving the army.

Mexico City. The United States gained not only Texas, but also all of the Mexican territory north of the Rio Grande, including what is now New Mexico, Arizona, and California.

At the war's end, Grant and his unit returned to the United States, and in 1848 he married Julia Dent in St. Louis. Military life, however, did not allow the couple to stay together long. Grant served at various military posts in New York, Michigan, Oregon, and California. With so much time away from his wife, he grew lonely and depressed and eventually decided to resign from the army. He returned to St. Louis, where he tried several business deals that failed. His next move was to Galena, Illinois, to accept a job as a clerk in his brother's leather goods business.

While watching the local militia on the parade grounds one day, Grant was asked to help out with their drill. The townspeople knew about his West Point and Mexican War experience. He accepted, and the militia improved at once as they followed his sharp, clear commands. Soon after, Governor Yates of Illinois requested that Grant accept an offer to become a colonel of a newly formed regiment, the 21st Illinois Volunteers. He agreed and from then on his fame grew.

Meanwhile, the conflict between Northern and Southern states was intensifying. Among other political disputes, the South's practice of keeping slaves was the main reason for hostilities. In late 1860, several Southern states seceded from the Union, or left the United States to form a country of their own, the Confederate States. President Lincoln began organizing the U.S. Army for war, and on September 4, 1861, Grant was put in command of the Cairo, Illinois, Union headquarters, where he had control over Southern Illinois and southwestern Missouri. It was with this assignment that Grant began to display his planning skill and his ability to carry out those battle plans and tactics, a talent that would bring him to the attention of the nation and, specifically, President Lincoln.

The shooting war had begun in April 1861 at Fort Sumter, South Carolina, and the tension was felt as far west as Illinois and beyond. There would be no more parades with bands playing—this was the real thing. While Grant disliked the agony and bloodshed of war he was now doing the very thing that his country had trained him to do at West Point.

With his step upward in military command Grant wasted no time in starting operations. His two main targets were Fort Henry on the Tennessee River and Fort Donelson on the Cumberland River, both considered vital in striking at the heart of the Confederacy in the western theater of operations. In these surprisingly easy victories, Grant earned a heroic reputation in the North, especially because he demanded complete, flat-out surrender from his enemy, with no favors and no requests granted. He became

Grant leading his men to victory
at Fort Donelson

known as "Unconditional Surrender Grant"—another nickname based on his initials, United States.

What kind of a man was Grant? He was far from a picture general, a parade ground dandy. His uniform coat was usually loosely buttoned, and his boots were caked with mud. He was a man who had the ability to do the best with the men and materials given to him. His manner was calm and determined, not one for strutting about and making a big show. He was a good family man and devoted to his four children, a decent man who was never heard to utter a curse word or tell a dirty story. His reputation was frequently marred by accusations of excessive drinking, but the charges against him were never substantiated. Among the men who served him, he was held with so much respect and admiration that they would follow him anywhere. He was indeed a "soldier's soldier."

The battles at Fort Henry and Fort Donelson were the first real victories for Union troops, but the next major battle at Shiloh, Tennessee (April 6–7, 1862), almost resulted in a defeat. It is said that Grant was caught napping by a surprise Confederate attack, and it was only through the arrival of reinforcements that his troops were saved. Fortunately for Grant, Lincoln did not lose confidence in him. He still believed that Ulysses S. Grant was the man who would instill a winning spirit of the soldiers of the Union forces. To prove this point, Congress made Grant a major-general and appointed him to command the military department of Western Tennessee.

Grant with some of his Union soldiers during
the Civil War in 1864

What a dramatic change in his life in only twelve months. From a clerk selling animal hides in Galena, Illinois, to a major-general commanding thousands of men. What a difference a year made!

One of Grant's biggest concerns was Vicksburg, a fortress on the Mississippi River that had to be taken if the Union hoped to split the Confederacy in two. It would be no easy task because Vicksburg was protected by heavy artillery batteries, and access from the north and south was almost impossible because of the heavily wooded swamplands.

A portrait of Grant, Commander and Chief Officer of the Union Army in the Civil War

Selected Major Battles of the Civil War

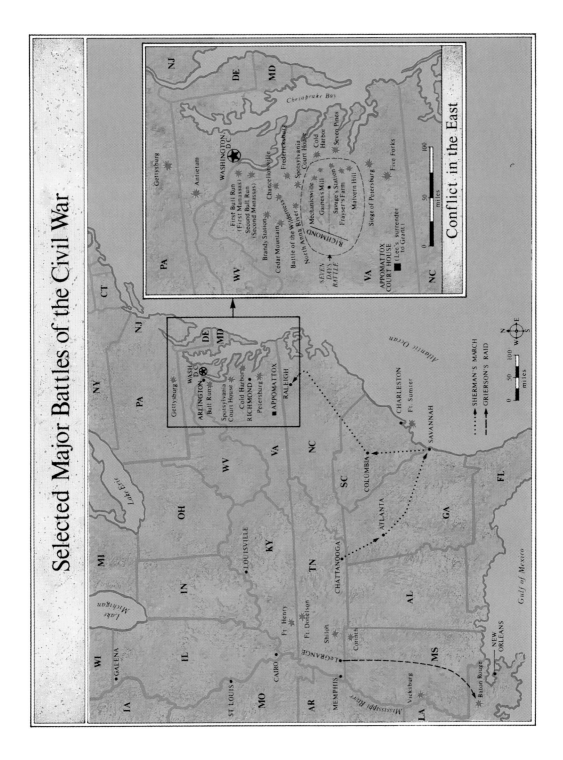

Conflict in the East

Confederate soldiers at the
Battle at Siloh

The seige at Vicksburg,
Mississippi

Several canals were dug in an attempt to bypass the large guns on the city's riverfront, but floods washed these out. The largest cavalry raid of the Civil War, known as Grierson's Raid, was made to divert the Confederate army's attention away from Vicksburg. Union Colonel Ben Grierson and 1,200 of his cavalrymen rode from La Grange, Tennessee, to Baton Rouge, Louisiana, passing through Mississippi, disrupting railroads and telegraph stations in their path. Meanwhile, Grant's troops fired on Vicksburg relentlessly. The siege lasted forty-seven days before Vicksburg finally surrendered on the morning of July 4, 1863. This split the Confederacy in half and assured Union forces control of the Mississippi River. President Lincoln summed it up by saying, "The Mississippi River now flows unvexed to the sea."

Lincoln appointed Grant lieutenant general, thus giving him command of all U.S. armies. Grant now put General William Tecumseh Sherman in charge of the western theater, and Sherman proceeded to march through Georgia and destroy the Confederate stronghold in Atlanta. Grant, meanwhile, went east to lead the Army of the Potomac in pursuit of Confederate General Robert E. Lee, whose army was the only force still propping up the South. Grant met Lee in a series of vicious, deadly engagements at the Battle of the Wilderness (May 5–6, 1864), Spotsylvania Court House (May 8–19), North Anna River (May 23–26), and Cold Harbor (June 3–12). Grant's forces con-

Grant planning the attack on
Cold Harbor, June 2, 1864

Grant and his generals in a painting
by Peter Balling, 1865

tinually suffered more casualties than Lee's, but Grant had far more troops in reserve. While he chased Lee through Virginia, Grant knew he might have been losing battles, but he was winning the war.

The last hope for the South was to defend Richmond, Virginia, the capital of the Confederacy. Grant felt he should first skirt south and take Petersburg, which would cut off Richmond's supply line. When he attacked at Petersburg in June 1864, he met Lee's strongest defense yet. The battle became known as the Siege of Petersburg and dragged on for ten horrible months. With his troops and the citizens of Richmond ill, tired, and dying of hunger, Lee finally tried to escape and join other Confederate forces. Grant pursued and pinned Lee down at Appomatox Court House. Lee's historic surrender to Grant took place on April 9, 1865, in a meeting between the two great generals. For a man nicknamed "Unconditional Surrender," Grant's terms were surprisingly lenient, allowing Confederate officers to keep their guns and personal possessions, and for every Southern soldier to return to his home unmolested. Grant even fed Lee's starving men from Union food supplies.

With Grant's defeat of Lee, the Civil War ended. All other Confederate forces quickly surrendered, and within weeks, the mighty task of rebuilding the nation was to begin.

Celebration at Grant's
triumphant return home
to Galena, Illinois, on
August 19, 1865

Above, Grant's home in Galena, Illinois, which was built in 1857. Right, The library of Grant's home in Galena.

Chapter Four

GRANT THE STATESMAN

On APRIL 14, 1865, U.S. and Julia Grant were to attend Ford's Theatre in Washington as the guests of President Lincoln. At the last minute, the Grants changed their minds and instead visited their children in Burlington, New Jersey. President Lincoln was assassinated that night, and as the nation mourned their great loss, General Grant was left to wonder if he might have been able to prevent John Wilkes Booth from shooting the president.

The new president, Andrew Johnson, had a stormy relationship with Congress, made especially bitter by Congress's rejection of Johnson's plan for Reconstruction of the South. Grant was a political ally of Johnson, but when

A poster of Grant and running mate
Schulyer Colfax during Grant's campaign
for the presidency in 1868

Johnson battled Congress over political appointments,
Grant resigned as Johnson's secretary of war, winning the
favor of many Republicans in Congress. Grant was subse-
quently the Republicans' presidential nominee, and in
1868, the great Civil War hero was elected the eighteenth
president of the United States.

Grant's inauguration as the
eighteenth president of the
United States, March 4, 1869

When Ulysses Grant took the oath of office on March 4, 1869, he was forty-six years old, the youngest man ever to hold the office. Bands played, troops paraded—it was a very exciting event. But Grant was elected during one of the most difficult times in American history. Severe problems still lingered over the Civil War, such as how to implement the abolition of slavery and rebuild the South's economy, which had for generations relied on slave labor. The United States's tense relations with American Indians gained prominence when General Custer was defeated at the Battle of the Little Big Horn in Montana. The national debt had become huge, and there were financial disputes with overseas allies.

When Grant changed roles from general to president he also had a change in life-style, yet he and Mrs. Grant and their four children, Frederick, Ulysses Jr., Nellie, and

Grant with his wife and friends on the
porch of Long Branch Cottage, 1875

Grant with his wife, daughter Nellie,
son Jesse, Jesse's friend Willie Coles,
and Ullysses S., Jr., at the Grant's
cottage in the 1870s

Grant's daughter
Nellie and her
husband, whom she
married while Grant
was president

Jesse, adapted quite well to their new home in the White House and remained the same quiet family as before. Grant had very little experience in governing and realized it. Yet he was determined to be a good president, and he was bolstered by his popularity with the voters and the recognition he received as a military genius.

As with other presidents before him, Grant found his first weeks in the White House to be full of changes, both social and political. He reasoned that if he surrounded himself with capable people and used his own knowledge of handling troops, he could manage the country quite well. In the early months of his presidency, Grant concen-

A presidential portrait of Grant
painted by Thomas LeClear in 1880

trated on things that he thought would benefit all the citizens and also have a lasting influence. Among his proposals that Congress enacted were establishing an intercontinental railroad and national park system. Perhaps the most significant accomplishment of Grant's presidency was in foreign relations. Coming into office, the United States was embroiled in a bitter financial dispute with Great Britain, but Grant settled the matter peacefully.

Grant easily won reelection to a second term in office. He was still seen as a national hero, a man admired by millions. Despite his popularity, his political career began to turn sour. His choices of some cabinet members and other administration officials proved to be mistakes. Grant's aide, Orville E. Babcock, was indicted for his association with an illegal "whisky ring" that sold liquor but defrauded the government of tax revenue. Secretary of War, William W. Belknap, was impeached for accepting bribes. Many people were surprised by some of Grant's choices to help run the government, but being a trusting person he expected this same quality in others. Critics often pointed out that two of Grant's weak points were in giving too much authority to others and trying to reward friends who later took advantage of him. He openly admitted that mistakes were made during his administration but that they were a result of political inexperience on his part, not of bad intent. All he could do was to shrug his shoulders and keep on trying as he had as a military man.

Chapter Five

WORLD TOUR

WHEN ULYSSES GRANT completed his second term as president in 1877, he was exhausted and disappointed that things had not gone well. Deceived by friends he trusted and tired of listening to critics, he wanted a change of scenery. He thought the answer might be to go on a journey abroad to places he had often heard about but never seen. Because he was now in a position to do anything he wanted, travel was his choice. Little did he realize that when he made the decision to do some traveling, he would wind up visiting forty countries on a worldwide tour.

He sailed from Philadelphia on the passenger steamer, *Indiana*, accompanied by his wife, Julia, and his youngest

**Grant receiving the Freedom
of the City of London award at
Guildhall in London, 1877**

son, Jesse, who was nineteen. His destination was Europe, with stops in England, France, Russia, Italy, and Spain, and then on to Asia to visit China and Japan. Grant's fame was far-reaching, and he was greeted by huge crowds at every port. Grant delighted in the opportunity to sample foods of the world, ranging from elegant French cuisine to the

Grant with Li Hung Chang,
the Chinese Secretary of
State, during Grant's visit
to China in 1879

exotic dishes of the Far East. Quite a change from his traditional American meals!

Finally, after more than two years of travel, his journey ended when he returned to the United States and landed in San Francisco, California, where another huge crowd greeted him with one of the biggest celebrations in history. After a brief stay that was busy with banquets and receptions, he then proceeded east by railroad to New York City. As his train passed through cities and towns the people gathered

Well-wishers greeting Grant in
Key West, Florida, 1880

A formal portait of
Ulysses S. Grant

to pay him tribute. The one big stop he made along the way was in Chicago, where another huge parade, led by his old friend and fellow soldier, General Phil Sheridan, was held in his honor.

The world tour had been a real boost for General Grant's self-esteem. The crowds anxious to see a famous man, welcoming speeches, awards, banquets all gave him a renewed feeling of importance.

Travel had been enjoyable, but he was now faced with two problems: where to live and how to earn a living. He solved his first problem by deciding to make New York City his home and bought a house there. The money problem would not be so easy because ex-presidents were not expected to start a second career. To make matters worse, he was swindled in a business deal by a man named Ferdinand Ward. Feeling desperate was quite a change for the man acclaimed a military leader, a hero to the nation, a man used to cheering crowds and well-wishers. But Grant was a determined man who had survived other critical times and figured he could handle this situation. The only trouble was that there were going to be even more difficult times ahead.

Chapter Six

FINAL YEARS

THE FEELING THAT he was entering another low point in his life was coming over General Grant. As a result of bad business deals he needed money. Also, he had developed a health problem, a painful disease in his throat that was later diagnosed as cancer. The money situation worried him because of his desire to provide security for his family, the most important people in his life. He was very proud of the fact that he had always been a good husband and father, a man who never used bad language and neither would he permit a dirty story to be told in his presence.

General Grant thought he might solve his money problem by writing a book. After all, he had much to offer

Grant and his family, including the
grandchildren, on the porch of his home

being a famous man in history, a man who played a big part in bringing the North and the South together again as one nation. In addition, he also had the rare quality of being able to get a message across in direct, plain, everyday language, an important factor in writing a book.

When Mrs. Grant heard of her husband's intentions she suggested to the General that they accept the offer of a friend who would let them use his cottage in upstate New York, where the cooler weather would make it easier for Grant to write. He agreed and they went by train to Mt. McGregor located near the town of Saratoga, New York. He started writing the manuscript in pen and ink, but later changed to pencil as the sturdy wooden pencil was easier to grip. His throat cancer was getting worse. Again, showing the same will and determination that he had always shown, he had made up his mind not to stop writing until he finished the book. The book, titled *Personal Memoirs,* was completed two days before Grant died. At the last, he was very weak and in a great deal of pain. His last written words were, "I hope no one will be distressed on my account."

Personal Memoirs proved a financial success, and provided his family with the funds he so sincerely wanted them to have. Interestingly enough, the owner of the company that published the book was one of Grant's old friends, Samuel Clemens, better known as Mark Twain.

The aged and ailing Grant writing
his memoirs in upstate New York

**The last photograph ever taken of Grant,
four days before his death**

Grant died on July 23, 1885, at age sixty-three. He had outlived his former war foe, Robert E. Lee, by fifteen years. As Grant's funeral train left upstate New York headed for New York City, it passed the United States Military Academy at West Point where the entire Corps of Cadets stood at attention and presented arms in a salute to General Grant. The cadet captain who called the corps to attention was John J. Pershing, later to become General Pershing, commander of all the American forces in World War I.

Grant's funeral procession in
New York City, August 5, 1885

When General Grant's funeral procession passed through the streets of New York City, an estimated one million people lined the 7-mile (11-km) route. The procession, led by President Grover Cleveland and members of Congress, was one of the greatest tributes ever paid anyone in the United States. The General's final resting place, Grant's Tomb, is the largest burial vault in America.

Grant's Tomb located on Riverside Drive and 122nd Street in New York City

For Further Reading

Cannon, Marian G. *Robert E. Lee.* New York: Franklin Watts, 1993.

Carter, Alden R. *The Civil War: American Tragedy.* New York: Franklin Watts, 1992.

Kent, Zachary. *Ulysses S. Grant: 18th President of the United States.* Chicago: Childrens Press, 1989.

McFeely, William S. *Grant: A Biography.* New York: Norton, 1982

O'Brain, Steven. *Ulysses S. Grant.* New York: Chelsea House, 1991.

Rickerby, Laura. *Ulysses S. Grant & the Strategy of Victory.* Englewood Cliffs, NJ: Silver Burdett Press, 1990.

Smith, Gene. *Lee & Grant: A Dual Biography.* New York: McGraw-Hill, 1984.

Ward, Geoffrey C., with Ric Burns and Ken Burns. *The Civil War: An Illustrated History.* New York: Knopf, 1990.

Index

About the Author

BILL BENTLEY holds a masters degree from Central Washington State University. He has been a career educator at both the public school and university levels of teaching, and is also the author of five books and more than sixty magazine articles. His interest in General Grant began in his native state of Missouri, where his home was located only a few miles from Grant's Farm in St. Louis County. He was inspired to write this book by this lifetime connection to General Grant, as well as his own military background that includes combat duty in the Pacific.